69 Buzzing Questions to turn your life Upside-Down.

Written By

Simone Vincenzi

69 Buzzing Questions to turn your life Upside-Down

Copyright © Simone Vincenzi 2013

First published 2013

Published by Simone Vincenzi

Email: simone@yourpowertoshine.com

Phone: 07912689219
URL: http://www.yourpowertoshine.com

All rights reserved. Without limiting the rights under copyright reserved above, no part of this publication may be reproduced, stored in or introduced into a database and retrieval system or transmitted in any form or any means (electronic, mechanical, photocopying, recording or otherwise) without the prior written permission of both the owner of copyright and the above publishers.

69 Buzzing Questions to turn your life Upside-Down

Vincenzi, Simone

ISBN: 9781492108900

Contents

- PREFACE……………………………..8
- INTRO…………………………….…..14
- *Ultimate Awareness*…………………..19
- *Explore Your Creativity*…………........81
- *Boost your Vibrations*……………......111
- *Massive Action*………………….…...135
- CONCLUSION……………………..152

To my family, friends, the people I met along the way and all the life experiences that gave me the strength to be who I am now.

In Particular to My Mum Rosaria, who always believed in me, despite my rebellious behaviour.

To my Dad Daniele, who taught me that change is possible.

To my dear brother Graziano, for accepting my escape from Italy. (Grazio we'll be together soon).

My dear friends Pino, Gibbo, Deolo, Il Cap, Il Put, Cassio and all The Pirate's Crew of Maranello to be always present in my life.

To John, Indio e Ste from the bar Pellini, who taught me how to be an excellent waiter.

To Pietro Fraccari, who taught me the road to happiness.

To Illa Kahgram, always ready to bring me down to Earth when my mind fly too high.

To my business partner Ben Shorter…. Mate You Rock!!

To the Clinton Swaine and the Frontier Family for pushing my personal and professional growth.

To everyone I didn't mention now, but I carry in my heart.

To God, for giving me the gift of life every breath of my life.

THANK YOU.

PREFACE

Hi, My name is Simone Vincenzi, I am an Inner Coach, Youth Coach, Entrepreneur and International Public Speaker.
Well... these are the labels I choose to give myself for the purpose of this book :)

I honor you and thank you deeply for taking the time for your inner growth.

I don't know who you are. I don't know where you are coming from. I don't know where you want to go.

But there is a thing about you I know for sure. Otherwise you wouldn't have bought this book.

I know that you are committed to your growth. I know that you are looking for something that is more than what you perceive. And I know that you are looking for practical tools that will help you living a more fulfilled, whole and successful life.

If you are not that kind of person, and this book was a present, I invite you to just pretend, while reading, to be that kind of person. It simply looks and feels cool!

Before we start, I want to answer to a question that maybe is popping into your head now.

"Who are you why should I trust you?"

Legit questions...

My name is Simone Vincenzi and I am originally from Italy. I was born in "the land of the cars" Maranello, a little town close to Modena and Bologna, famous for being the place where Enzo Ferrari and the car that wears his surname was born.
I grew up in a loving family with my mum, always caring and giving and my dad a hard worker and committed to the family. We were blessed with another member few years later. My "little" brother who is now bigger than me.

Obviously like everyone involved in personal development I faced a lot of challenges (learning opportunities) in my life. I know each one of us could write a book about our life and inspire people with their stories.

Well, this won't be the platform where I am going to share my challenges as a whole and how I overcome them.

But my promise is to inspire you with the tools every day that took me from being a waiter who could barely answer a phone call in English in the restaurant where he worked, to being founder of two successful businesses and an international public speaker at 24 years of age.

If you will confront this book with an open and inquisitive mind and be receptive to the simple but effective tools I am going to share in a moment, you will be willing to turn your life upside-down in a snap!

I want to share with you something funny about the title. Maybe it is one of the reasons why you decided in first place to pick up this book.

69 is a number very dear to me for several reasons which I am not going to explain in detail.

One of these reasons is that it was the result of my final exam at secondary school.
What is so special about it?
In Italy the exams rate goes from a minimum of 60 points to a maximum of 100 points.

I was always the very smart guy that didn't want to study and lost focus very often. (A lot of entrepreneurs can relate with this spreading disease). So the commission of teachers decided in advance that they would let me pass the final exam with the bare minimum, (like saying finally we got rid of you!!). But I surprised them by creating one of the most original theses they received. So they decided to increase my score. They were looking for a number between 68 and 70. Then My Philosophy teacher Sonia Righi, which I deeply loved from the first moment I saw her, proposed the magic number to the commission stating : "Let's give him *69*! He will be proud of his score for all his life!".

And here I am now, writing about it and creating a personal development book around this number!
Sonia... You knew me very well!
This is my gift to you.
This is what I have learned by the most influential people in personal development like Tony Robbins, Brian Tracy, Ben Shorter, Elliot Kay, Steve Beckles-Ebusua, Clinton Swaine, Illa Khagram and many others who have guided me as coaches or mentors through my journey towards the successful life I am living.

I was asking myself what did they have in common and I found out that all of them are able to change their state by asking themselves powerful questions.

I wanted to learn from them and I have been applying these questions to my life, which helped me facing the challenges I had, from homelessness, to food addictions, to complete lack of money.

But you know what I am talking about, don't you? If hadn't had had those challenges I wouldn't be writing now to you this book. And you if were not facing some challenges right now or had some major blocks in your life, I am sure you would not pick this book up.

Am I right or am I right?

INTRO

The reason why I am writing this book is because I want you to understand the real power of questions and the role they play in shaping our destiny and our life.

As Anthony Robbins says, our thoughts create our emotions, our emotions create our actions, our actions create our destiny.
I believe nothing is more true.
If we look at the scientific side of it, Neuroscience has demonstrated that our thoughts trigger the amygdala, the centre of our brain that controls our emotions. Every time a thought is fired up, the amygdala, looking back in its emotional database, recreates an emotional state that is related to that thought.

Can you follow me?

So we can easily say that if we can control our thoughts, we would be able to control our emotions, our actions and our destiny.

But what is a thought and where does a thought come from?

I am going now to answer those questions that have been crossing my mind for months.

A thought is an answer.
A thought is an answer to a question we consciously or subconsciously ask ourselves. Imagine your mind to be like Google. What do you do when you want to find an answer in Google?
You type a question, don't you?
Do you agree that the more specific is the question you type in, the more specific and detailed is the answer you can find?
I am sure you do!
Great!
A thought is the same. A thought is an answer to a question we ask ourselves.
When the question is specific and well-formed, the answer is a quality answer, when the question is not clear and empowering, the answer is not useful at all!

Now, let's get back to the thought loop I introduced at the beginning of the chapter.

Can we say now that the questions we ask ourselves determine our thoughts, our thoughts determine our emotions, our emotions determine our actions and our actions determine our destiny, can we?

Can you understand now how crucial it is for your success, in every area of your life, to understand how to use this fantastic tool called mind in the most effective way?

This is why I decided to put together the questions I met along my coaching career that made a massive impact in my life and the life of the people I coached.

But I wanted to dig deeper, and I wanted you to understand what happens to our mind, body and spirit when we ask some of those powerful questions.

Some of the questions I am going to share with you have the power to raise the vibrational frequencies of your energetic body so you can elicit emotions inside you that will allow to manifest faster and clearer the reality you want to create.
How does this sound to you?
The following questions have been proven and tested by thousands of people and by my personal experience.
I have personally chosen the questions that I ask myself on a daily basis as soon as my worries or challenges take over my positive state.

I have been practicing them for years and I want you now to own this powerful tool that can change the way you live your life and outcome you reap on a daily basis.

The reason why all the questions are written using the second person is because, mentally, allows you to dissociate with the current situation. This helps you to be detached from your feelings and emotions, in particular in the case of a challenge or an unexpected situation in your life, and allows your Shining Self to give you the answer you most need in that moment.

I decided to group the questions in 4 different categories so, every time you find yourself in the middle of a challenge, you will have the right question to use to cope with the moment.

The categories are:

Ultimate Awareness

Explode your Creativity

Boost Your Vibrations

Take Massive Actions!!

Ultimate Awareness

1. What do you really want now?

Behind every emotion lies a desire. This question is designed to find the underlying cause of your feelings. When you are feeling upset, angry, sad or disappointed, ask yourself "What do you really want now?" and listen to your inner voice. In this way you will shift the focus from a feeling of lack to a feeling of power. Aligning with the desired object and connecting with its energy. It is very useful to shift low vibrations into higher vibration.

2. What is it that you are really looking for now?

This question explores the object of your desire and targets your focus to the real reason for the emotional experience. It is very useful to use when uncertainties and worries take over your natural, harmonic state of being.

3. What is stopping you now?

This question shifts the focus from an internal perspective to an external perspective, inviting you to see the reality of the obstacle for designing the best strategy to play with it.

4. What is most important for you here?

This question is crucial in decision making. It helps eliciting or raising the awareness of your priorities, so you can make the choice that is serving you the most and plan your actions accordingly.

5. What is it that you value the most about this?

This question is crucial in decision making. It helps in eliciting or raising the awareness of your values, so you can make the choice that is serving you the most, in alignment with your core values, preventing self-sabotaging behaviors and allowing you to live in flow.

6. What do you believe to be true about this situation?

This question is designed to explore your perception within your internal reality, digging into your belief system and firing the light on your current thought process. Awareness is the #1 key for change. This is the #1 question to ask yourself every time you want to explore what is happening within your ears on a belief level.

7. Where does this belief come from?

This question has been tailored to elicit the origin of your current belief. Limiting or empowering beliefs are formed by the people around us and society in our early childhood. With this tool you will be able to re-connect with the moment where your belief has been instilled, leaving you freedom of choice. Be still and listen to the answer. Listen to the first answer that comes up from you.

8. Is this belief moving you towards or away from your goal?

This question is destined to reconcile your quest for clarity. Stephen Covey in the 7 habits of highly effective people says that habit 1 is: "Begin with the end in mind." Now with your goal in mind ask yourself if this action is in alignment with where you want to be. If yes, keep going!! If the answer is NO... well... the choice is in your hands!

9. What have you done today to help you move closer towards your goals and dreams?

This question is perfect as a goodnight question to check within yourself what steps you have taken during the day towards what is important for you. If every single action is in alignment with your vision... well... You are a master!!

10. What can you do tomorrow to help you move closer towards your goals and dreams?

This question is perfect as a goodnight question to set up your subconscious mind for the actions to complete in the day to come. Our subconscious mind is always working. If you ask yourself this question before going to sleep, your mind will work on the best strategy for you to follow through the task you have planned for the day.

11. How is this action aligned with your values?

This question is ideal for decision-making. Always check what you value the most in this area of your life and decide if the action is in alignment with your core. If not... well... you know already what to do, don't you?

**12. How is this question aligned with your
purpose?**

Great question for an inner check! Once you have re-connected with your unique purpose in life, it is always crucial to check if what you are doing is not just aligned with your values, but also with the reason why you are here on this planet. If the check is positive for both: my friend you are in!

13. What will happen if you keep taking this action?

How would you feel in 5 years' time? This powerful question has been extensively used in the Dicken's Process designed by THE COACH Tony Robbins. It works effectively as it projects the mind into the future, exploring the consequences of the current action. Will you regret it or look back at it with gratitude? The choice is yours.

14. How are you really feeling about it?

Get in touch with your gut. Get in touch with your feelings. What are you really feeling about what is happening in this moment? Be honest and true with yourself and do not pretend to feel differently. In every single feeling there is a meaning meant to be explored.

15. What does this mean for you?

After connecting with your feelings, now it is time to understand the meaning that brings the feeling into your awareness. Listen in silence for the first answer that is coming up from your heart. Do not judge it. Just accept it.

16. What is the learning in this for you?

This question forces you to shift your level of awareness from the problem to the learning for you that is wrapped in the problem, allowing you to act from a place of resourcefulness instead of being a victim.

17. What inspires you?

Life is boring if you choose to make it boring. Understand what inspires you and do more of it. Your life will be a playground of meaningful experiences!

18. What is your big WHY?

Ask yourself what is the motivator of your life. Your life is the meaning you choose to label it. Live from a place of inspiration and you'll be able to inspire others and make this world a positive place to live in.

19. What is your biggest passion?

Do you want to live a life full of colours or just different shades of grey? Connecting with your biggest passion allow you to colour every single day of your life with what you love the most. What are you waiting for? Go and do it!

20. What is your life worth living for?

This question allows you to connect with what is important for you. What is that gives a meaning to your life and gives you a reason to wake up in the morning?

21. What is worth dying for in your life?

Now that you know what it is that moves you to live every day, it is time to connect with what is the reason why you will sacrifice your own life. What is the call, bigger than you that can move you even to give up the most important thing you have? The answer is extremely connected to your Life Purpose.

22. What is your vision for the world?

This question invites you to think about the ideal world you'd like to live in. The world you'd like to leave to your children and grandchildren. This is an invitation to think about your role in the creation of this world. What part are you willing to play to make this world a reality?

23. What is your purpose in life?

BIIIIIG question!!! Now it is time to explore the reason why you are here on this planet. Each one of us has a unique purpose in life. Achieving and living your purpose is allowing yourself to live in alignment with your Shining Self. Alignment means abundance, fulfillment, love and joy in each area of your life. Are you up for connecting with all this?

24. What is your mission?

This question is designed to help you think about your mission. Your mission is the tool that you will use to live your purpose. It is the "What" you are going to do to make your purpose a reality. For example my purpose is to support people to re-connect with their Life Purpose and with the Confidence and Power within themselves. My mission is to coach them towards this awakening. Coaching is what I use to live my purpose daily, now reflect. What is your Mission?

25. If you had a friend who spoke to you in the same way that you sometimes speak to yourself, for how long would you allow that person to be your friend?

Now it is time to boost your confidence, stop your disempowering talk! Often we are our worst enemies and we keep repeating, like a broken record, everything that ever had an influence on our life. Most of the time they were not the nicest things and we keep living this programme over and over again. When you change the way you talk to yourself, you will change the way you live your life.

26. If you have to give your grandchildren 3 pieces of advice about life, what would they be?

This question is studied to allow your mind and heart to connect with what is your message. What is it that you'd like to share with the world, that you have learnt from your unique personal experience, in order to empower other people. Let's get this message out there as much as you possibly can!

27. If you had a message to share with the world, what would this message be?

This is the one thing you'd like the world to know. Starting from your personal experience, what is it that can empower, inspire and support people all over the world?

28. What is it that makes you really happy?

Happiness is a conscious choice. Happiness is the result of your choice to be happy, no matter how life is treating you. Connect with what makes you happy and do it every day! Music, art, a walk, love? Choose your way towards happiness.

29. What is it that makes you really angry?

This is a great question to realise consciously what is pushing your buttons. What is it that you cannot really stand in life. Now ask yourself "What is about it that makes you really angry?" and find the pattern. Self-awareness is the first step towards enlightenment.

30. If you had to let go of something in your life, what would you let go of?

Negative people, events and circumstances can affect our present and our future beyond our current awareness. It is your responsibility to create a space within and around you that will lead you to your growth and not to your stagnation. Now it is time to let go of what served you in the past but is not serving you anymore.

Explode your Creativity

31. What else can you do?

Let's stre-e-e-etch your mind. Think beyond the limit. We live in a Universe of infinite possibilities. Do not limit yourself to the first thing you can think. Allow yourself to be bold, creative and brave

32. What can you do to feel more active now?

Energy is what keeps you alive. Energy is what keeps you in flow. The more energizing things you do, the more life will flow into you, the more you will flow in life. Find what boosts you and do more of it daily.

33. What do you need to overcome this obstacle?

This question allows your mind to take a different perspective about a problem. Visualize the problem like an obstacle along your path and explore all the possible solutions you can think of and choose the one that resonate the most with you.

34. What would the person you admire the most do in this situation?

Great question to outsource solutions from the field. In this way we channel into the energy of the person we are thinking about, living or dead, and we channel their thoughts, emotions, feelings and patterns. Practice it often and tune into the energy of the person you admire the most. Whatever comes up will make perfect sense for you.

35. What belief and thought can be more useful for you in this situation?

We are in control of our reality by choosing the meaning we give to our experience. We choose this meaning from our thoughts and beliefs. Now it is time to choose consciously what patterns can be more useful for you in a challenging situation.

36. Who can you support achieving this goal?

It is not just about your personal goals and vision. Tailor your goal towards an outcome that can serve other people as well as you. If everyone could do it, what kind of world would it be possible to create?

37. What is the best question you can ask yourself now?

This question invites your mind to connect with Your Shining Self. Through this question the mind surrenders to the heart, asking for guidance and direction. A powerful question that can trigger the mind again to find the best solution.

38. What would you do with your time if money wasn't involved in the equation?

Now think about what would really add juice to your life. What is that you would love to do, day after day that brings light to your life. Always follow your passion, overcome the limitation of your mind telling you that "you cannot afford it" or that you don't have the time to do it". This question is designed specifically for me and is the one, which I struggle the most to apply.

39. How will your life be in 5 years' time if you take this action?

Every action you take is the seed of an outcome. What do you want the outcome to be? Give up the end results but know within yourself you have done the right thing

40. What can you do differently now?

Albert Einstein said: "Insanity is doing the same thing over and over again and expecting different results." If you feel stuck in the same cycle of patterns, do something different and break the pattern. The end result will change consequently.

41. What would you like to feel now?

The emotions that we feel create the reality we perceive. Create emotions within yourself that can empower you, moving away from your limitations. Choose the emotion that will eventually create the end result you are looking for.

42. What is the feeling that can move you closer to where you want to go?

Think now about the feeling that will create the reality you want to live. Tune in with yourself and connect with the feeling that can give the desired end result.

43. What is Your Shining Self saying now?

Inner check! Your Shining Self is always communicating with you via your emotions. Tune into your emotions and listen to what Your Shining Self wants you to know. By just listening and caring about Your Shining Self you will create a supportive relationship with yourself.

44. IF THERE WOULD BE A QUESTION THAT COULD TURN YOUR LIFE UPSIDE-DOWN WHAT WOULD IT BE?

Questions are a tool for creativity. Be creative with what you ask yourself and experiment with the different answers that are coming up in your mind. If you are looking for change and you want to turn your life upside-down, this is the question you are looking for. It will trigger the train of thoughts designed to give you the answer you are looking for. Then narrow it down and ask yourself the question that comes up for you. Then TAKE ACTION!

Boost your vibrations

45. I know you don't feel this way now, but how would you feel if you were/ had...?

My favorite question! This question is so powerful because it allows you to acknowledge your state, creating no conflict between your experience and the expectations of the mind. Then it lowers the emotional pressure creating a situation in possibility. This question is able to deceive the conscious mind, getting straight into the subconscious which cannot distinguish between reality and possibility, enabling you to elicit your desired emotional state.

46. Is it going to be important in one year's time? If Yes, what changes can you make right now? If No, how can you get over it?

Most of our worries and arguments are generated by the conflict between the expectations of our mind and the current reality. Our mind activates the fight or flight response which, releasing stress hormones, creates a state in our body where we are focused on our "survival". If the situation is really major and will create a negative impact in your life in the span of 1 year, YES, do something about it. If not... well… Let it go!

47. What can I do to show you my love?

This is a question to ask yourself as often as you can possibly imagine. While I am writing this book I have a lot of resistances coming up and distractions that are limiting my work. I know that my inner child is looking for attention now and I ask myself this question to show love and care to myself and to calm my inner child. Also self-love is the most powerful healing tool you can use for healing your life.

48. How would you feel if you were thinking this way all the time?

This question is designed to lead you to explore your inner feelings about your current thought process. Every thought we think creates feelings that trigger the release of certain hormones in our body. Most of the time we are not trained to be aware of this process and we are not in tune with the real feelings that our thought process can trigger. Asking this question to yourself helps you stepping into your real feelings and guides you toward re-patterning the thoughts that serve you no longer.

49. What are you most grateful for in your life?

Gratitude, one of the most powerful emotions humans can feel. The emotion of gratitude, as clearly explained by the spiritual teacher Abraham Hicks, it is the emotion that can bring us in touch with Source and works as a magnet for positive things to happen into our life. Make a daily habit to list what you are grateful for in your life and send to the Universe those positive vibes. The Universe will indeed respond back with the same energy multiplied.

50. What would Love do in this situation?

Powerful question to step into the consciousness of Love. We have the power to channel external answers, tapping into different energies. If it sounds too woo-woo for you, I invite you to do some research and find out more about this great tool that we have. Love is the biggest power in the Universe, Love is the energy of God. Tuning into the personified consciousness of Love is tuning in the personified consciousness of God. Make peace within you and listen to the answer. You know it will be the right answer.

51. Why are you abundant in your life?

The following questions are designed to deceive your conscious mind and go straight to the subconscious mind. As stated before a thought is an answer to a question that we ask ourselves. Generally speaking the question WHY? Is a question that we, as coaches, avoid because it triggers the mind to find a justification for the fact. But we can be smart and use this process to empower us instead of dragging us down. As you can see if you ask yourself: "Why am I abundant in life?" The mind is engaged in seeking a solid justification to confirm the fact. This tool, taught to me by my spiritual coach Illa Khagram, founder of Radiant Lotus, is more powerful than affirmations themselves. If you are using affirmations for your life you'll be impressed by the results you will achieve using these questions!

52. Why are you beautiful as you are?

53. Why are you so smart?

54. Why are you so sexy?

55. Why are you so brilliant?

56. Why is your life so wonderful?

57. Why are you so lucky in life

58. Why do you have everything you need right now?

59. How old would you be if you didn't know your age?

I am not going to spend much time on this question. I invite you to feel it inside you and come up with your answer. I believe we are ageless and age is just a number printed on documents socially accepted as regulations. I am not asking you how old your body is, but how old are you?

60. How would you feel if you were the most important person in the world?

Now imagine being the most important person in the world. How would you walk? How would you talk? How would it be? How would you feel? Connect with those feelings and images and start creating this confident map of yourself for a brighter and more fulfilled future.

61. What are the blessings in your life right now?

This question re-connects you with the feeling of gratitude within yourself. We are all blessed in our life but sometimes we let the expectations of our mind displace the countless blessings that are given us each given moment. Now re-connect with those blessings, and if you are facing a challenging period, see it as a gift. Challenges are opportunities given by God for our growth.

Massive Actions

62. What are you waiting for?

Get in touch now with your emotions. If you want to make that change or do that thing... well, what are the excuses you are making to yourself about why you cannot do it. Start giving yourself the excuses of why you can do it.

63. How can you apply those learning now?

This question puts you in the driving seat. From learner to master. Just taking actions and doing what you learn you will achieve life mastery. Now think about how you can become a master and all the possible ways you can apply in life what you have learnt.

64. What can you do to serve other people today?

This is the most powerful question you can ask yourself. I personally do it every morning as soon as I wake up. Then I create some silence within me and listen to the answer. We are here for serving. We are here to serve and grow. Think about all the different ways you can serve humanity today.

65. What can you do today that will make a massive impact in the world?

Now, think about your actions as a tool to make a positive impact in the world. Do not worry if the current action does not seem to be creating something positive. But having this as an end goal in mind, you will see that your actions will be guided from a greater power. You will know (or not know) later the ripple effect that your activity really produced. Quoting Steve Jobs: "One day you will connect the dots."

66. What are the 10 most important things you can do tomorrow before 10am?

Achievers wake up early. Well, we can debate about this one. I had a very interesting discussion with my business partner Ben Shorter who loves working during the night. I learned this from the Success Coach Bill Walsh and I applied it to my life. Every night I go to sleep with this mindset I do at least 8/10 of the things that I plan. The bottom line is to prioritise what are the most important things to do in your day and do them! The rest will fit in like rice fits in the middle of stones in a jug.

67. What can you do now to get you closer to where you want to be?

Now, still with your end goal and vision in mind, take action on what moves you forward in life. It can be just a simple email or changing the environment you are in if it saps your energy. Do something for your goals every day. My business partner, Peak Performance Coach Ben Shorter, is the living example with his "NO DAYS OFF THEORY". It does not mean have no rest. It means take actions towards what is really meaningful for you.

68. What are you going to do today with your time?

Your time is the most precious thing in your life. It is not true that time is money, money is time. Money is the result of the time you spent and invested in your activities creating a change in people's life. If you spent meaningful time, you will reap meaningful money. Also we cannot buy time and every second wasted is a precious second of our life. Be mindful with your time and use it wisely for the good of humanity.

69.

What can you do to reward yourself today?

CELEBRATION! Celebrate your success and do something for yourself every day. This is called positive selfishness. Do something for you that is so meaningful that you will be filled up with the right energy that will allow you to serve and support others. Remember, you are the most important thing in your life.

CONCLUSION

In this book You have learnt and used for your benefit the 69 most powerful questions you can ask yourself.

Thank You for allowing me to guide you through this journey and I guarantee that the more you use this tool and see this book, the more the use of these questions will become second-nature, use the book every time you feel the need of support.

An effective way to use this book, if you believe in synchronicity, is to set an intention for your outcome, take a deep breath, close your eyes and trust that the right question is the one that is manifesting to you in that moment.

For any further enquiries, comments and recommendation, feel free to contact me at simone@yourpowertoshine.com and I'll do my best to personally respond to you.

Also if you want to know more about what I do, you can find me on www.yourpowertoshine.com, my blog and on my youtube channel.

May your life be filled with meaningful questions.

Simone Vincenzi

Made in the USA
Charleston, SC
10 January 2015